Dedicated to my mother who gave me the strength and wisdom to look at the world around me. Finally to my loving family, and my husband David, who have supported me in my quest to compile this book of poetry.

Karen J Burns

CHAOS: MAY THERE
YET BE HOPE

AUSTIN MACAULEY PUBLISHERS
LONDON * CAMBRIDGE * NEW YORK * SHARJAH

Copyright © Karen J Burns 2025

The right of Karen J Burns to be identified as the author of this work has been asserted by the author in accordance with sections 77 and 78 of the Copyright, Designs and Patents Act 1988.

All rights reserved. No part of this publication may be reproduced, stored in a retrieval system, or transmitted in any form or by any means, electronic, mechanical, photocopying, recording, or otherwise, without the prior permission of the publishers.

Any person who commits any unauthorised act in relation to this publication may be liable to criminal prosecution and civil claims for damages.

A CIP catalogue record for this title is available from the British Library.

ISBN 9781037104268 (Paperback)
ISBN 9781037104275 (ePub e-book)

www.austinmacauley.com

First Published 2025
Austin Macauley Publishers Ltd®
1 Canada Square
Canary Wharf
London
E14 5AA

A big thank you to Austin Macauley for all their hard work in getting this collection of poetry to publication. Thank you for believing in my ability as an emerging poet, and for allowing me to get me poetical expression out to a wider audience.

Also thanks go to Patricia Wilmott who created the Cover illustration (turning my idea into something visual); to Dr Gascoigne- who's advice to keep being radical, will always inspire my writing, to poets who have inspired me- Michael Rosen, Pam Ayres and the late Benjamin Zephaniah (May he rest in peace).

Finally a big thank you to all those who have been following my poetry journey- your support, feedback, and love has made a real difference. I know that you will be eager to see what the future brings; and I shall keep writing poetry to inspire, educate, and make a bit on sense in all of this chaos.

Never give up hope!

Table of Content

Introduction	9
Chaos?	11
Angry at the World	13
Campaign of Fear	14
Poor Sacrificial Lambs	15
See Their Evil	16
Welcome to Planet Fear (Aka Twisting the Narrative)	17
Stoking the Victim Blaming Fire	18
Villains and Heroes of Power	20
Who Should You Fear?	21
Their Prey	22
Welcome to Post-Tory Britain	23
A Few of the Tories Favourite Things	24
A Few of Labour's Favourite Things	25
Don't Drink from Their Poisoned Chalice	26
End Stage Capitalism	27
Where Olive Trees Weep	28
Fear Less	29
Us to Blame?	31
A Hard Pill to Swallow	33
A Better Way	34
A Moment of Contemplation	35
Broken Britain	36
Beyond Repair, Or Care	37
Beware Liars and Thieves	38
Chaos Reflected	39
Distract the Masses	40

Forgotten Values	*42*
Hating on truth	*43*
Heads in the Sand	*44*
Hidden Beneath	*45*
Humanity's Earthly Doom	*46*
Kindness Not Hatred	*47*
Lost Freedom	*48*
Hope Out of Despair?	**49**
Hope Out of Despair	*51*
Count and Share Your Blessings	*52*
Changing Narratives	*53*
Calmly Does It	*54*
Be on the Right Side of History	*55*
Avert Away from Evil's Glare	*56*
I'm a Dreamer	*57*
Utopian Resolution	*58*
Awaken from Slumber	*59*
Aura Of Calm	*60*
Brighter Days	*61*
Easter Call for Peace	*62*
Down Not Out	*63*
Changing Reality	*64*
Cherish Today	*66*
Weaving Us All Together	*67*

Introduction

Chaos: May There Yet Be Hope appeared out of the backdrop of the pandemic, a time of great reflection. Fresh out of university, with a head full of ideas and dreams, I sat down and started letting all my thoughts rush onto paper.

Chronic illness came along, throwing an obstacle in my path that I couldn't have imagined in my wildest of dreams. Yet out of the gloom of despair, came a plethora of poetry. My daily writing soon became a cathartic way to deal with the challenges, that life with pain, was throwing at me.

I soon connected with other like-minded poets and discovered a whole world of enlightened creatives. This network of creative minds, spurred me on, to write more and more. I was encouraged to share the words that had once been in my head, and found an audience that could relate to my thoughts and musings.

Largely, my poetry is inclined towards a sociopolitical nature; which I blame on my sociology-based degree, and my time at Warwick University. A truly inspiring time that I will not forget, for as long as I shall live. I am truly grateful to my personal tutor, Dr Stephen Gascoigne, who told me to always be radical; and to NEVER dumb down my writing.

Finally, whilst I am sure my poetry can be likened to Marmite; love it or hate it, as some may. I am sure that there are plenty of people who can resonate with my words. Poetry like song, has the power to reach into our hearts.

Chaos?

Angry at the World

I am angry at the world today.
At those letting values slip away.
And the leaders who wilfully,
Brought us all this decay.

I am shouting at the people,
Who failed to see the powers' plan.
Crazy blinkered people,
With their heads deep in the sand.

I am crying at the suffering,
Vulnerable people taking the brunt.
Whilst some entitled people,
Keep voting for greedy cu**s.

I am praying for the world,
That it might see the light.
And for hope and determination,
To wake them to fight.

Campaign of Fear

Around the country, they chart their course,
A rainbow of colours, for one force.
Riddles and myths, to spin their tale,
To keep this illusion without fail.

With a backdrop of despair, they travel far,
Their corruption is hidden behind battle scars.
On choppy waters this boat set sail,
All aboard a fateful campaign trail.

Promises and pledges are doled out like candy,
Distractions are more than a little bit handy.
Blinkers are an optional accessory to wear,
But personally, I need to scream, I swear.

And when the day of reckoning is here,
Just how many will survive, or disappear?
In this game Wack-a-mole,
Is it us or them that gets to be consoled?

And though this force, may bear another name,
Its ideological intentions stay the same.
No matter the sailor designated to steer,
He'll whip up a storm, a campaign of fear.

Poor Sacrificial Lambs

Twisted, gnawing, and pitifully bleak,
Weakened, vulnerable souls they seek.
Erosion of hope, through their narratives of fear,
Left with no paddle, unable to steer.

Battered and bruised, left with no fight,
We sit meekly and consider our plight.
Sat in a cavern, awaiting a rope,
People so desperate, unable to cope.

Caught in their headlights, deer in a trap,
Woefully awaiting the sound of the snap.
Yet, their false promises, see us fall for scams,
We're broken, discarded, poor sacrificial lambs.

See Their Evil

Turn your heads, avert your eyes,
Mute the sound of their cries.
Do not trust your vision,
For evil's not their decision.

Block out their double speak,
For it's you that's bleak.
Lost your mind,
They're not unkind.

Hey, are we mad?
Or could it be that we are sad?
Weeping at the stark corruption,
That is wrought by such destruction.

Yet lacking the power to stop this game,
Evil played out in religion's name.
Hating their scapegoating ways,
That covers up their power play.

A veil to hide the truth, to hide their wrongs,
Twisting the attitudes of everyone,
Crazy words obscure their meaning,
Yet it's not us that's dreaming.

We see this nightmare playing on,
Knowing just who power wants gone.
And we knew it all along,
Now we choose to ignore that it is wrong.

Or we can open our eyes,
Shout out, drown out their many lies.
Lend our voices to the weak,
To crush the evil power seeks.

Welcome to Planet Fear
(Aka Twisting the Narrative)

Welcome to Planet Fear!
Buckle up for the journey,
It's going to be a bumpy ride.

Putin's got his finger on the button,
And Netanyahu's really a nice chap.
And the Pope's not catholic.

Sunak's helping our nation flourish,
And Starmer's providing an opposition.
Democracy is alive and kicking don't you know.

Biden's memory is fine,
And Trump's all that we should fear.
But Harris is better for the white house, now it would seem.

Nuclear war is around the corner,
Climate change is just a hoax.
Barmy weather is all-natural, nothing to see here folks.

Are we crazy? Mad or stupid?
When we swallow all these lies.
Or do we wear an invisible cover? That covers up our eyes.

Stoking the Victim Blaming Fire

Stoking the fire of victim-blaming
Directing attitudes through its framing
Reality mirrored into something fiction
Hard watching brutal male rape depictions.

Pre watershed show attracted many a complaint
pretty pictures their narratives did not paint
Victims focus, feeding into survivors' worst fear
Men still hold all the power or so it would appear.

Creating awareness with the best of intentions
Taking onboard abuse charities' suggestions
Mindfully underlining issues of consent
Yet gaslighting was all too evident

Believable characters did well in to display
The aftermath of those who did stay
Differing attitudes Ben did find
Friends and family who were not all that kind

Ben's masculinity placed on display
Toxic questioning in a way
Hardman image reminder so stark
A nod to his father, it does mark
Asking questions about Ben's victim status
When throwing his violent nature at us
Beating up guys twice his size
Making vulnerable Ben seem like lies

Whilst victim's emotions came from a heinous crime
His abuser exited at the very same time
Though this scenario too often rings true
A different ending was important too

For awareness is no good on its own
When toxic maleness is not shown
Empowering survivors to find their voices
Eastenders should have shown us other choices
It really isn't the dramatization that is told
But the power of a male-led society that's sold
Victim-focused depictions inevitably stay
Instead of challenging toxic masculinity that refuses to go away.

Villains and Heroes of Power

In the realm of British politics, a tale unfolds,
Where characters emerge, their stories bold.
A landscape of intrigue, power, and strife,
Where villains lurk in the corridors of life.

Beneath the grand façade of Westminster's halls,
Lies a cast of characters, where ambition calls.
Like fictional villains, they try not to get caught,
Their intentions hidden; their desires sought.

In the heart of power, where agendas clash,
Political foes engage in a cutthroat dash.
Like Voldemort, seeking ultimate control,
Some politicians strive to conquer that role.

Others, like Cruella, with scheming fights,
Care not for the consequences, nor the people's plight.
Their thirst for power knows no bounds,
As they navigate these political battlegrounds.

Yet amidst the darkness, often heroes emerge,
Champions of justice, their voices surge.
Like Harry Potter, they fight for what's right,
Standing against corruption, with all their might.

In the tapestry of British politics, with villains abound,
May Heroes rise, with virtuous sound.
May the light of truth shine through the fray,
And guide us all towards a brighter day.

Who Should You Fear?

There's a familiar rumbling,
In the corridors of power.
A rattling of sabres,
From their ivory towers.

History doesn't repeat,
People are guilty of this.
As well as being blind,
To all that's gone amiss.

Swallowed up by myths and fables,
Entrenched in ideological lies.
Fed a mass of entertainment,
Its only job is to disguise.

We're played like a fiddle,
By an orchestra that's well-versed.
With their sights on the money,
In a mission that was rehearsed.

Nothing is an accident,
In this theatre of power.
Because as they rise above us,
It's us who must bow down and cower.

And whilst it may sometimes seem,
Like it's for our own good.
I would ask you to be unblinkered
And take off that mythical hood.

Wake up to all the lies,
Question everything you hear.
And ask yourself this question,
Who is it you should fear?

Their Prey

Power is like a bird in flight,
Soaring above, with eagles' sight.
Searching for the weak and easy prey,
Those through policies they can slay.

Circling in flocks to show their might,
All in protection, in case we fight.
Gorging on all the spoils of our land,
In their missions, they had planned.

Hoarding and robbing, as per their type,
And feeding us all with their lying tripe,
And when these birds have had their fill,
They'll crush us down and render us still.

There is no escape from their evil claws,
As they have us trapped by all their laws.
And the power is stolen by twisted words,
"It's for your own good," laughed the mockingbirds.

Welcome to Post-Tory Britain

Welcome to post-Tory Britain,
Where corruption knows no bounds.
Lying and thieving politicians,
Where no morality can be found.

Partying during lockdown,
Whilst we all stayed at home.
Rules not for them,
As they were left to roam.

Chucked money at their buddies,
Whilst saying there was none.
Yet always money for wars,
Can I hear you say, how come?

They defended known sex pests,
Yet said others are a threat.
Like the MP that joined Labour,
Just in case you forgot.

We have all heard of the knighthoods,
Which clearly can be bought.
In a nation with many foodbanks,
Perish the actual thought.

And now as another era has started,
We wait with trepidation.
For another round of promises,
And more crooked explanations

A Few of the Tories Favourite Things

More empty rhetoric
Than ever before.
Vile hate narratives,
We all should implore.
These are a few,
Of the Tories' favourite things.
MP corruption,
Giving money to their mates.
Depriving the many,
Left Britain in a state.
These are a few,
Of the Tories' favourite things.
As the race starts,
And the mud's thrown,
We'll be spun a yarn.
And now as Election Day, has come and gone
When will they ever return?

A Few of Labour's Favourite Things

More broken pledges
Then ever before.
Vague empty promises,
Hide what's in store.
These are a few,
Of Labour's favourite things.

MPs swapping sides,
Interchangeable at will.
More Tory deflections,
Are expected still.
These are a few,
Of Labour's favourite things.

When the race starts,
And the mud's thrown,
We'll be spun a yarn.
And now the election has come and gone
Will the future be good or bad?

Don't Drink from Their Poisoned Chalice

From the poisoned chalice of politics, we drink,
Wondering just how low they'll make us sink.
Marketed to appear like a palatable blend,
Just how far will their deception extend?

Yet signposted to look the other way,
By distractions which woefully led us astray.
Feeding us with fear to keep us compliant,
Because otherwise, we might become defiant.

And when their poison becomes too vile,
Too much for the many to reconcile.
They'll find a new scandal to distract us more,
In their attempt to even up the score.

Like it's all a game of seeing who's worst,
To stave off the inevitable, the bubble gets burst.
Dragging our nation into the pits of hell,
So, if our system collapses, we do as well.

All designed to prop up their greedy ways,
Inequality is waged, in this game they play.
Flipping the narrative, criminalizing the poor,
Switching the people we're meant to deplore.
A veritable deception in front of our eyes,
And powers immune to our screams or our cries.
Full speed in their mission to full social control,
They seek to own minds and our very souls.

Yet there is still time to wake up to their lies,
Take off our blinkers, get back control of our eyes.
And clean the wax from our ears, to hear the truth,
Listen carefully, we can hear the proof.

And we can regain all they wilfully stole,
Get back what was lost, and regain control.
Joining together to make society strong,
Just as we should have done all along.

End Stage Capitalism

RIP to the Labour Party,
Welcome to one-party state Britain,
Where actions aren't matched,
By the words that are written.

And democracy died too,
Now no more than a lie.
It's the narrative they tell,
That's pure pie in the sky.

End-stage capitalism's,
Final curtain.
When will it collapse?
Well, I can't be certain.

But this ideology,
It can't be sustained.
Under the same rules,
Or the same game.

For this game of chance,
Is running out.
Affecting their proponents,
Alienating the devout.

But without our money,
The system has nought.
It's to our consumer choices,
Our voices are sought.

So, shout out loud,
And bring on change with your voices.
If like me, you hope.
To see new future choices.

Where Olive Trees Weep

In the heart of biblical lands,
Much war is raging.
At the heart of power,
Greedy minds are engaging.

In a land of oppressed people,
Where mercy is lacking,
Genocide is allowed,
Because justice is slacking.

In the place where Olive Trees grow,
Destruction's causing much pain.
Truth hides behind fear,
Distraction away from whoever gains.

Weeping olive trees front their cries,
No masking horrors, no act of disguise.
Yet though visual, there are muted pleas,
Crushing of souls, at the hands of the thieves.

Fear Less

Ribbons and buttons,
A haberdashery smile,
Perfectly crafted, by a long mile.
Practical decorations, well well-packaged placements.
Hidden within the depth of our basement.
All manner of scraps,
And material pieces.
All mixed with remnants of Reece's Pieces.
An era of memories, wrapped up into one
From a bygone era that's long gone.
At the same time,
Just as these flashbacks appear.
I hear a noise that fills me with fear.
A scratch then a squeak, distracts my mind,
What cretins lurk to blow my mind?

A little searching,
Revealed a pair of twitching faces,
I'm ready to flee, as my heartbeat races.
But then I stop, and reconsider my fear,
As I wipe away a lone straying tear.
No more afraid of what lurks beneath,
In the darkest depths under there.
They've no more places to hide anywhere.
All horrors uncovered in the blink of an eye,
Illuminated by a cracked portal to the sky.
With no more reasons to take flight,
I marvel at all that time forgot.
All the hidden gems that weren't liked a lot.
And as it all swirled around my mind,
I wondered why I left them behind.

My youthful days,
Not so much a haunting curse.
More a drumming rhythm and verse.
This happy place brings back my smile,
The briefest comfort, by a long mile.
And as I stare at these forgotten gems,
Covered in dust and waiting to be found.
In their tomb capsules underground.
I make a pact to revisit my past,
To reveal the part of me I'd masked.

Us to Blame?

A Hard Pill to Swallow

Lies are more palatable than what's true,
When blissful ignorance consumes you,
For in a world of make belief
Fantasy is one of far less grief

When we swallow their half-facts
Allows them to cover their real tracks,
Distorting history as it goes
Defines the enemy, such deceit bestows

Creates an image of division and hate
Pits each country and each state
Centres our hopes around one common focus
Through this patriarchal lying circus

Yet in our obedience to our state
Sees them seal our eternal fate
Though blissfully ignorant I am not
Their regulatory positions see me rot

My eternal hope rests in my demise
My faith in God I won't disguise
Whilst there are those of wilful pretence
Their lies will be their recompense

Although it may seem like lies are winning
As foretold from the beginning
Cometh a time when the truth will out
Exposing the truth of the lying lout.

A Better Way

A tip for a world that's struggling,
And that's trying not to drown.
A way to save each other,
By lifting, not trampling down.

A request for a way of kindness,
Of empathy that understands.
Instead of people who harm,
One that holds out its hands.

And when we're all feeling selfish,
Competing against our friends.
Let's flip out our attitudes,
To reverse these selfish trends.

For all humans are capable,
Of living a different way.
In putting others before them,
When living there day to day.

So, as you face the world,
Stepping out on this fine morning.
Do your best to herald,
A new world that could be dawning.

A Moment of Contemplation

Silence fills my cosy space,
A warm and comfortable place.
Where troubles seem so far away,
Hoping behind doors they'll stay.

Flitting through socials, fingers are itching,
Try not to engage in vast hate-filled bitching.
Distraction techniques that polarize our views,
Propelled around platforms like actual news.

TV Avoidance, escape from news,
Focused on doom, does not amuse.
Too many channels, paint a fake story,
Rewriting history, with its slant to glory.

Yet a lightbulb moment, gets me thinking,
How my noisy mind sees me sinking.
Overthinking harms, here in my quiet space,
Wrecks my calm, my mind's all over the place.

But what's the solution? to save my sanity,
In a world of chaos and increasing vanity.
What's the way to live in calm?
To block out all that does us harm.

Broken Britain

Rotten apples in an orchard,
Soiled our nation to the core.
Robbed the funds of the poorest,
Yet their greed saw them want more.

Wars and evil are their focus,
Whilst the poor are left to die.
Making money for the wealthy,
Whilst the rest are left to cry.

No shame has these politicians,
As they play out their wilful game.
Leaving us people all to suffer,
This Broken Britain shame.

Beyond Repair, Or Care

Britain broken as it can be,
A right fatality.
People are beyond correction,
No hope of resurrection.

Woefully they deflect,
Their lack of respect.
And it's oh too plain,
This ever-growing stain.

Like a messy forgotten yard,
That society wilfully disregards.
Head turned another way,
By what leads them all astray.

Shiny bling is their new saviour,
In this unpalatable-looking flavour.
Many hearts are eroded by its draw,
And their minds sink and hit the floor.

What's the betting there's no way out,
From this ill-begotten drought.
No help for those without care,
Who will fatefully die just there?

Beware Liars and Thieves

From the liar's playbook,
The newest scam unfolds.
A black hole of missing money,
The myth we're being sold.
But look here comes a story,
Gifts for favours, all the same,
A game of deception, by another name,
To confirm the crooks, they are.

A veritable Robin Hood, but in reverse,
As lower and lower thievery sinks.
This game of fear control,
Designed to erode our souls.
And there's only one way,
To win the war they waged.
It's through our unity,
And not through our rage.

Chaos Reflected

Grey wash-over kind of day,
In an era-reflective, kind of way.
A mirror to the dreary outlook sees,
Yet it's us that caused this ugly.

Mixed up seasons, crazy weather,
We shifted course and slipped the tether.
Nature inflicted chaos, with no return,
Yet we weep as we watch it burn.

Our tears so sodden, add to the flood,
Blindfolded to see we're stuck in this mud.
Stuck in this cycle, rinsing of gloom,
Full speed ahead to our actual doom.

With warnings aplenty, ignored by greed,
It's evil persuasion, our fatal seed.
We purchased our blinkers, sold out our fate,
Our hope's now beyond that pearly gate.

Yet fog set in, obscuring that heavenly direction,
And an array of words, our misdirection.
Befuddled messages, racing madly around,
It's no wonder we've run aground.

And the way back, a veritable reboot,
But are we willing recruits?
Can we take off those blinkers?
Shift our minds and be reasoned thinkers.

Are we comfy in this disorganized room?
Stuck in our chaos, in our acceptance of doom.
Scared of the light, we won't make the exchange,
Stuck in a rut, we're unwilling to change.

Distract the Masses

The ways of the world, well there are many,
Common as muck and ten a penny.
Plenty of fads, a Tik-Tok explosion,
The normal thought process, a fateful erosion.

Multiple memes fly around the web,
Distraction for the unsuspecting plebs.
Oh, what a hoot, a bit of fun,
Let's all ignore that smoking gun.

Cheap entertainment available on tap,
Yet it makes me want to scream and slap.
Or shake some sense into conforming sheep,
Apathetic people who've gone to sleep.

Football crazy, and media mad,
Yet care less for war, and that is sad.
Passions rise at all wrong things,
While Gaza weeps, England joyfully sings.

And as I lay detached from this madness,
My heart is consumed by reality's sadness.
By blocking out fake joy's gladness,
My eyes are open to all the world's badness.

Yet I ponder on what tomorrow might bring,
When voices quieten and no longer sing.
Like a firework, it fizzles to nought,
A disappointment for some, I have no doubt.

Fear not, this calm will not last,
Await another resounding blast.
Olympic fever is on the way,
Distracting mailable minds, to make their day.

Constant distractions to keep us back,
Keep us in line, and on the right track.
Controlling thoughts, whilst saying we're free,
I hear you say, oh seriously!

But stop for a moment and consider this,
Is all this nonsense really such bliss?
And when stripped away, what's left?
In a world so broken, and sadly bereft.

Forgotten Values

In life, there are many mysteries,
Puzzle pieces are out of place.
Inequality and injustices,
In our living breathing space.

Myths and slogans there are many,
Designed to sway us from the proof.
Yet even seasoned socialists,
Have missed the actual truth.

Knowing Attlee and Bevan,
Were purveyors of all that's good,
But the faith that stood before them,
Is not widely understood.

Oh, too quickly they've forgotten,
The Christian ethos of the day.
When too readily they'll follow,
To push that God away.

Yet socialists aren't alone,
In their confusion of the past.
For Christians aplenty,
Also leave me much aghast.

How can any believer,
Be captured by the cruel?
Right-wing followers,
Igniting greed's fuel.

If Jesus was alive,
He'd love and feed the world.
Preach truth to all the people,
And lift the vulnerable and unfurled.

Hating on truth

Are we stupid? Or just mad.
Or perhaps sad? That we're not glad.

Is there something in the water?
Or maybe just distracted by the TV.
Are we lost in all this fiction?
Or just can't stomach to know the truth.

Perhaps we lost our sense of ability,
Thrown all rational thought away.
Chucked all reason in the dustbin,
Preferring our fairy tales instead.

Heads in the Sand

Thoughts all lost and carried away,
The people are lost in their day to day.

Aspirations are fine but centres on thee,
The plight of others you do not see.

Words get lost in the recesses of minds,
The lies take over one surely finds.

Like a flamingo with its head in the sand
Our nation of people so sadly stands.

Hidden Beneath

Murky sludgy deepest grime,
A mixture of mud and leafy slime.
Sediment that lies beneath it all,
In the hidden depths of nature's call.

Silence hangs like it's missed a beat,
Deep down in this, the river's retreat.
A place so detached from all life above,
Dingy and gloomy, devoid of light's love.

And though a creepy place to be,
Its beauty is in its solitary, you see.
Set apart from a world so unkind,
What's hidden beneath, one cannot find.

Yet out of darkness comes new living seeds,
In its glorious and awesome-inspired breeds.
The eggs of feeders that like the forbidden,
Not repulsed by the gloom, in their quest to stay hidden.

And as I think of this watery, murky zone,
I contemplate its type of home.
Away from a world that seems so devoid of love,
In this lucky escape from the chaos above.

Humanity's Earthly Doom

Fluffy clouds sitting proud up in the sky,
Evil and unkindness have made them cry.
Bucketloads of sorrowful tears,
For an outpour of destruction, done over the years.

Rivers spill and soil the faultless earth,
Shameless in their pitiful worth.
Changing a landscape created by greed,
Selfish attitudes were that seed.

Crops and fauna all purposely destroyed,
Through policies arrogantly deployed.
The irony of capitalism, too stark to ignore,
Yet arrogant man refuses to see what's in store.

Nature's suffering at evil greed's hands,
Really against any sustainability plans.
Progress, full speed destruction,
Woefully by mankind's own instructions.

Topsy turvy way of humanity's thinking,
Mankind will be the ones left sinking.
Because in this game of win or lose,
It's us that capitalism really screws.

Nature's power mightier than the sword,
By its destruction, we can ill-afford.
Humanity's going to be the ones weeping,
Nature's killing them whilst they were sleeping.

End times are fearfully around the corner,
How many will be petrified mourners?
Or how many will transcend to a better place?
Where tears of destruction don't fill that space.

Kindness Not Hatred

Words so cruel and unkind,
It doesn't help mankind.
Words so ugly and vile,
Such awful rotten bile.

Attitudes so vicious,
Shows humanity as malicious.
Narratives of hatred and disgust,
Sees us fatally combust.

This propensity for greed,
It only makes us bleed.
Selfishness that harms one another,
Destroying our earthly sisters and brothers.

Can we let kindness win?
Shift away from all our sins.
Loving-kindness sees us winning,
A chance for hope and a new beginning.

Lost Freedom

In the days of old, when children played outside,
In lovely meadows, in long grass, they'd hide.
With wildflowers blooming, such a pretty sight,
Watching bees galore, do a happy flight.

Yet time changed our nature, in the most awful of ways,
Because of the way we chose to live out our days.
Meadows got scorned, by narratives of imperfection,
A move that took humanity in the wrong direction.

But as nature fatefully began to dwindle,
A return to wilding was slowly rekindled.
Proffering hope to our wildlife once more,
But what was lost cannot be restored.

Alas, by these tales of wildflowers, so grand.
Humanity will learn, all our future planned.
No changing direction, or going back to the past,
And when the rot sets in, the tide will turn fast.

And we'll find the outcome, of a poisonous seed,
The folly of our ways, the true cost of our greed,
Our wings ever clipped, and doomed like the bees,
All rights will be lost, and we'll never be free.

Hope Out of Despair?

Hope Out of Despair

Withered and gnarled
Feeling broken inside.
Twisted and decrepit,
Not a path I did decide.

Bruised and scarred,
Imperfections have marked.
Trauma and disruption,
On the journey I embarked.

YET

Glowing and radiant,
Warmth from the heart.
Hope and vision,
Sees gloominess depart.

Determined and strength,
Clear as water to see.
Inspires and promotes,
A brighter future for me.

Count and Share Your Blessings

The pace of life does seem crazy,
In who it leaves behind.
Yet the greed of the wealthy,
Means too many do not mind.
A cavernous void, for those called lazy,
With few hands to lift them out.
When alright jacks have plenty,
They care little for those with nought.
Empathy lacking, apathetic souls,
Blinded by selfish greed,
Have lost the ability,
To share with those in need
Narratives of competition,
Knocked their kindness away.
Changed their life's direction,
And led them all astray

Be not like these unkind people,
Proffer a hand to help the poor.
For tomorrow has not yet come,
And you don't know what's in store.
Life changes on a hairpin,
your luck could turn around.
Fame and fortune today,
Tomorrow could run aground.
Feel grateful for your blessings,
Leave jealousy at the door,
Share good fortune with each other,
And stop perpetually wanting more.

Changing Narratives

With eyes that see the horrors,
And ears to hear the truth.
Mouths to voice reality,
Propaganda hides that proof.

With minds that can decipher,
And hearts to feel the pain.
Greed came along to silence,
It's a wonder what it gains.

With influence in our words,
Creating talk of fear or hope.
With phrases that can rescue,
Or become our fatal rope.

With attitudes that can change,
Bringing about a world of peace.
If only we would question,
We could iron out this chaotic crease.

Calmly Does It

In the calm of gentle waters,
Quiet thoughts slowly flow.
Like a collection of quarters,
Left to multiply and grow.

A silent wish into a fountain,
For the water nymphs who knew.
Or a gentle sense of contentment,
In the gratitude which grew.

Like the mountains and their splendour,
Or a tall statue that's so strong.
A wall that will not crumble,
For it was solid all along.

And memories they do weaken,
As the wall comes tumbling down.
Like the fishy in those waters,
I swam, I didn't drown.

Be on the Right Side of History

Wake up, wake up,
Shake those blinkers loose.
Arise and smell the coffee,
Stir yourself and see the truth.

Wake up, wake up,
Time to tune out all their lies.
Take away the filters,
That hide and disguise.

Wake up, wake up,
Wash the dirt off your face.
Remove all the fakeness,
That aligns with their disgrace.

Wake up, wake up,
Clear the dust from your eyes.
Time to see who really wins,
And who's really left to cry?

Wake up, wake up,
Time to put your differences aside.
Time to join with one another,
To be on the right history side.

Avert Away from Evil's Glare

Never strong when we divide,
Gaslit to make us choose a side.
Fed a yarn, that tells a story,
Twists and bending history.

Words designed to wipe out doubt,
See all the reasons pushed right out.
Flipping morality on its head,
Good people must watch where they tread.

What's the purpose of this mission?
What becomes of this division?
When we're fighting to survive,
Fighting their evil to stay alive.

How do we rise from our pit of despair?
To live a life away from evil's glare.
To turn our backs on the populists calling,
When on our knees, pain sees us crawling.

Bravely we peer above their lies,
Breaking the fear that mutes our cries.
Letting integrity be our guide,
So, truth and honesty can reside.
And once we step out and take a stand,
We'll reduce the evil they had planned,
Or strengthen us to get through,
Through love and kindness, we grew.

I'm a Dreamer

I know that I'm a dreamer,
Hopeful for a Socialist way.
Imagining a parallel world,
Where greed no longer stays.

I know that I'm a dreamer,
Hoping for a world of peace.
In which capitalist destruction,
Is firmly told to cease.

I know that I'm a dreamer,
Wanting a home for everyone.
For inequality and poverty,
To woefully be gone.

I know that I'm a dreamer,
Seeking to wipe out all divisions.
For racial, cultural, sexual, and religious,
Hatred to be eradicated, by our wilful decisions.

I know that I'm a dreamer,
When I seek a world that's fair.
I may as well start wishing,
That our world's not round, but square.
If only our imagination,
Could become our reality instead.
No longer would I be a dreamer,
When hope replaced my dread.

Utopian Resolution

In this dystopian climate of fear,
Where darkness grows year by year.
Crushing our hopes and dreams,
No going backwards it seems.

In this land no longer great,
Where hatred wins to seal our fate.
Destruction and wars, oh what a state.
See some praying as we wait.

In these times we gave up the fight,
Where our buckling bones confirm our blight.
Greed replaces light to be the new shiny,
Shrinking our minds until they are tiny.

In this dystopian reality we face,
Wars and killing become commonplace.
Chasing away our hopes of salvation,
By destroying our wonderful creation.

In this the final days of this year,
Could we find a way to chase away fear?
A way to give darkness the boot,
Ejecting it from the lives it does loot.
In our hearts, we have the solution,
Could we make this our resolution?
To show dystopia out the door,
And herald Utopia in once more.

Awaken from Slumber

Time to wake up from your slumber,
Take off the blinkers that obstruct your vision.
Open your eyes to see their evil,
Their wilful destruction, deliberate decisions.

Time to realise what side they are on,
In their self-interest, they think they've won.
Yet we are many, whilst they are but few,
And by our eye-opening, we can renew.

Time isn't linear, it's full of disruptions,
So, we can disrupt their wilful corruption.
Humanity's good at rising to the occasion,
All it takes is some compelling persuasion.

So, my plea to you all today,
See the corruption that exists today.
Make a pact to work together,
To free Humanity from evil's tether.

Aura Of Calm

There is a force field,
It surrounds me.
Like a magnet,
It repels.
Pushing away,
All negative energy.
Yet drawing in,
Love and Kindness.
It's not a barrier,
More like a filter.
Sieving out toxic,
Unhelpful behaviour.
Leaving behind,
A sense of calm.
An aura of peace,
And a contented me.

Brighter Days

The warm-o-meter's topped up,
And the cold's packed up and gone.
Misery walked out the door,
And a sunny gladness won.

Warring ways remain the same,
And Biden's still clinging on.
But windy days have ceased for now,
And it feels like hope has won.

Food prices may still be rising,
And the bills are ever high.
But warmer days will be welcomed,
As the wonderful perfect sky.

Easter Call for Peace

In the quiet of Easter's dawn, a tale unfolds,
Of a love unbounded, a truth retold.
Beyond the chocolate eggs, beyond the feast,
Lies a message of peace, a divine release.

In the heart of Easter, Jesus' embrace,
A call for love, a sacred space.
Not just a story of crucifixion and pain,
But of resurrection, where hope reigns.

Amidst the turmoil of the Middle East's plight,
Easter's message shines a guiding light.
A call for a ceasefire, a chance for peace,
For violence and hatred to finally cease.

In the land where Jesus once trod,
Let Easter's message be a call to God.
A reminder of love, forgiveness, and grace,
A chance for healing, in this sacred space.

So let us remember the true meaning of Easter,
Not just chocolate eggs, but a love that's deeper,
May the Middle East heed this call divine,
And embrace peace in this sacred shrine.

Down Not Out

We Brits have had our fill
Of politicians who lie at will

Those dreams are in demise
By elitist greed that we despise

Our legacies and future stands
In these profiteers' grimy hands

Yet us Brits we can fight back
Show them we won't take this flack

Owing it to those not yet alive
To show that we can yet survive

They may think they have us beat
A turning tide sees them retreat

Just the beginning, not the end
It's our rights we defend.

Changing Reality

No more time for clutter,
Or for useless things.
No use for all the chaos,
Nor for overpriced bling.

No spoons left for fuss
Or endless stress.
No use for the judgy,
Heads that are messing.

No wish for noisy neighbours,
Or phones that ring all day.
No need for nagging people,
Nor a bitchy kind of way.

Yet…

A ton of space for kindness,
The vastest vessel of calm.
Plenty of plans to pace,
To protect myself from harm.

A life experience for intuition,
An abundance of common sense.
God's boundless amount of grace,
Made me strong, to lower that fence.

Add…

An increasing supply of contentment,
And gratitude, like an overflowing spring.
A smile that promotes much gladness,
Joyful as the birds that sing.

Because…

My life's a work in progress,
I will write as I go along.
Mistakes are all my challenges,
To learn from all that's wrong.

Each stage is like a chapter,
I can't wait to turn each page.
And I am its central actor,
Content to be at centre stage.

Life's also like the seasons,
And though winter is on its way.
I revel in autumn's beauty,
Cherishing each colourful day.

No more worries come to a burden,
Nor anxiety that drags me down.
And I know if I am hopeful,
Joy won't let me drown.

Cherish Today

Lots of things seem so stupid,
Until they really aren't.
Although they seem impossible,
There's no such word as can't.

In a world of so much chaos,
Order feels confined to yesterday.
Any sign of a progression,
Comes at a cost so steep to pay.

All hope seems just so battered,
Like fish washed up on a beach.
Yet the hope of our salvation,
Is so clearly within our reach.

Never fear for days unknown,
Or a past that took its toll.
For the future's yet unwritten,
And it is out of our control.

Worry not for tomorrow,
Let hope guide you along the way.
Creating memories designed to cherish,
And a life lived day by day.

Weaving Us All Together

More similar than we will ever know,
But how to make this common factor grow?
When polar attitudes pull us apart,
We need to dig deep into our hearts.

All wars and destruction need to end,
And loving hands need to extend.
Friendship bonds, where division hates,
Come on people, let's change our fate!

Our earth has resources that we all need,
Plenty for all, if it weren't for greed.
If only justice was there for us all,
Came to our rescue, and answered our desperate call.

And as I ponder this long-living conundrum,
I despair at those who think this humdrum.
Weep at the apathy that entrenched our hate,
At the people who shrug off their fate.

BUT WAIT

There must be a way to plant a sharing seed,
To weave solidarity, a new loving human breed.
Creating fairness and equality, ridding all hate,
A one-world structure to clean up this state.

Karen J Burns is a graduate of sociology, who channels her emotions and sociopolitical knowledge into her poetry. She started seriously writing poetry in 2021, just as the pandemic was calming down. Poetry became a cathartic way for her to express her view of the world we live in. It has helped her to make sense, in her own way, of this chaos.

Karen J Burns is a Christian, with chronic illness, who strongly believes that there is always hope, no matter how dark our world may be.